Grace

God's Unmerited Favour

"Let us therefore come boldly unto the throne of grace, that we may obtain mercy, and find grace to help in time of need"
[Hebrews 4:16].

B.Y. Stuart, PhD LCPC
Inspirational Series for Personal Development

May God's rich grace abound in you
Barbara
2012

Grace for Everyone
God's Unmerited Favour

*"For the grace of God that
bringeth salvation hath appeared
to all men…"*
[Titus 2:12].

Grace
God's Unmerited Favour

Copyright © 2009 B.Y. Stuart, PhD LCPC

Copyright © 2009 B.Y. Stuart, PhD LCPC

Faith Restoration Ministries Inc. [FRM]
www.faithrestorationministries.web.officelive.com

Printed in the United States of America
ISBN 1449594050

Salvation by Grace

"For by grace are ye saved through faith; and that not of yourselves: [it is] the gift of God:
Not of works, lest any man should boast"
[Ephesians 2:8-9]

Grace
God's Unmerited Favour

Scripture references used in *Grace* are from the King James Version of the Holy Bible.

Some verses were paraphrased for clarity, and not actual. Therefore, citations are at the end of related sentences.

B.Y. Stuart
2009

Table of Contents

Preface

Grace: God's Unmerited Favour exposes this spiritual virtue by explaining the *purpose* and *value* of this gift to God's people.

The book tells us that Grace goes beyond reciting, *"Grace is God's unmerited favour."*

There is much more to grace than God's favour.

Grace by itself, has a multi-faceted value which encompasses all other virtues or qualities a true Christian should possess.

Without the virtue of grace, it would be hard to maintain the daily Christian walk.

We need God's grace for everything.

God's grace will take us wherever He chooses, if we let Him.

Grace will keep us in any and every circumstance we face on this Christian journey.

Part I

Themes

This Section contains the following Topics:

1. What is Grace?

2. Grace: God's Unmerited Favour

3. Redemptive Grace

4. Amazing Grace

5. Christ-like Grace

6. Enabling Grace

Chapter 1

What is Grace?

We can all recite grace as *"God's unmerited favour."* Yet, is this all there is about grace?

Does grace means more than just favour to flaunt any way we wish without taking time to think seriously about this great kindness from a Holy God?

Is grace license for sin because it is available? [*See Romans 6*].

Let us take a deeper look at the word "grace" and the virtues it displays in the life of the believer.

Grace means mercy, *beauty, loveliness, being merciful, pleasantness, affectionate, regard, attractiveness, kindness, favour, charm* and much more.

Additionally, grace to the believer means God's unmerited favour.

The acceptance of God's grace declares us righteous in response to the Holy Spirit's conviction of the heart.

When we willingly embrace God's free salvation of grace through faith, this act frees us from the penalty of sin making us righteous before Him [Romans 3:24].

From the believers' position, grace demonstrates *patience, character, dignity, meekness, strength,* and *refinement.*

In fact, grace will help us to display all the fruit of the Spirit with the enabling power of the Holy Spirit.

Grace changes us from who we used to be to what God wants us to be as born again people.

Grace is the reflection of the Holy Spirit's work and presence in the life of the believer in Christ.

We cannot live righteously and godly in this present world without the evidence and operation of God's grace in our lives.

The walk of Christianity would be impossible for us if we had to depend on natural sustenance to make the journey a successful one in the end.

Grace enhances the believer setting him or her in a place of confident trust and faith in God.

The fruit of the Holy Spirit is indeed the work of Grace.

Each day allow this virtue to abound and excel in your life.

Chapter 2

G-R-A-C-E

1. **God's Grace** refers to His Unmerited favour. It is His free and merciful compassion and forgiveness towards us.

    God sent His Son Jesus Christ into this world because of His great love toward a fallen race [John 3:16; Ephesians 2:4].

2. **Redemptive Grace** - this is the free salvation given to us through the death of Jesus Christ. We are saved by grace through faith in Jesus Christ [Ephesians 2:8].

3. **Amazing Grace** – this is special favour, which makes us think of where we were before we received salvation.

Amazing Grace reminds us of what God has done for us while we were yet sinners and separated from Him [Ephesians 2].

4. **Christ-like Grace** is Self-discipline, and compassion [I Corinthians 9:27].

    It also includes Christ's humility [Philippians 2], compassion, love, and concern for people [Mark 8:1-9], and his selflessness [II Corinthians 8:9].

5. **Enabling Grace** is administrative grace. I believe we operate more in the *Christ-like* and *enabling graces* than we do the others.

    Enabling grace makes us merciful and kind to others, even when they offend us.

    We are constantly in battle and this requires God's enabling grace to overcome temptations, in order to go through trials [Ephesians 6:12-18].

Chapter 3

G

God's Grace
His Unmerited Favour

"But God, who is rich in mercy, for his great love wherewith he loved us" [Ephesians 2:4]

"...gave his only begotten Son, that whosoever believeth in him should not perish, but have everlasting life" [John 3:16].

"By whom also we have access by faith into this grace wherein we stand, and rejoice in hope of the glory of God" [Romans 5:2].

When we reflect on grace as God's unmerited favour, we must recognize it as special favour without the expectation of a return from the recipient. Favour means it was given freely.

All God requires is for us to receive the gift of grace through faith.

Sending Jesus Christ to die for sinners was God's expression of *immeasurable* mercy, and *unconditional* love [John 3:16].

This was great grace because we were dead in trespasses and sins [Ephesians 2:2-7].

Grace brought salvation to everyone who will believe and accept it.

We were far away from God and did not deserve His mercy or love.

In fact, we were in bondage to sin as prisoners of Satan.

Yet, God sent His Son Jesus Christ to redeem us from that penalty and to set us free.

God's unmerited favour was the merging of mercy and love, which began in the Garden of Eden.

It was after man's fall that God killed an animal and used the skin to cover Adam and Eve's nakedness.

They became naked when they disobeyed God's commandment [Genesis 3:21].

The sin of disobedience strips us from the covering of God's protection. It leaves us in spiritual darkness and weakness.

When the couple sinned and became naked, God showed great compassion and forgiveness towards them.

It was in the Garden of Eden where the first expression of love, mercy, and forgiveness were displayed for the remission of sins, by the shedding of blood.

This act of God saved Adam and Eve from eternal separation from His presence.

Similarly, Jesus' death and the shedding of His Blood covered our sins and reconciled us back to God.

Blood sacrifice began in the Garden and ended with the death of Jesus on Calvary's Cross.

Although the couple violated God's covenant; through His mercy, He had compassion on them.

Today that mercy and compassion have been extended to us through Jesus Christ, giving us access to this great grace through salvation.

"For by grace are ye saved through faith..." [Ephesians 2]. If Jesus had not come, we would have no hope.

However, God's grace, through the channels of salvation makes the difference.

God expresses this grace by sending His only begotten Son into a world of sinners, that whosoever believes on him should not perish but have everlasting life [John 3:16].

"Whosoever believes" does not sound like an expectation of return.

Therefore, "believe" is the condition and "everlasting life" is the offer.

The consideration is the benefits from the relationship the new believer will receive.

This contract is complete when the sinner repents and accepts Jesus Christ from the heart.

God gave His forgiveness, mercy, love, compassion, and kindness for us to accept or reject, and does not force His grace upon *anyone*.

God's unmerited favour [grace] is His expression of love and mercy towards us, which He freely gives to all who willingly receives this precious gift.

Chapter 4

R

Redemptive Grace
Salvation

"Being justified freely by his grace through the redemption that is in Christ Jesus [Romans 3:24].

"For by grace are ye saved through faith; and that not of yourselves: it is the gift of God" [Ephesians 2:8].

God's redemptive grace is a special gift. This is the gift of salvation, which came through His only begotten Son Jesus Christ [Romans 3:24].

Salvation is payment of a ransom to deliver, recover, rescue, or to set someone free.

It was redemptive grace, which acquitted us because Jesus became the *propitiation* [I John 2:2] for our sins.

Disobedience results in God's anger.

In order to pacify this wrath a sacrifice was needed.

Jesus became the Supreme Sacrifice whom God recognized and accepted because of His pure untainted blood.

All the blood sacrifices before Jesus' advent could not satisfy God's anger.

According to the Word:

"For it is not possible that the blood of bulls and of goats should take away sins" [Hebrews 10:4].

Therefore Jesus' blood was the only solution for sin, which God would accept to appease His anger since His blood was *"...without spot to God ..."* [Hebrews 9:13-14].

Only the blood of Jesus Christ is acceptable in the presence of a Holy God to purge us from the dead works of sin.

Before we accepted Jesus Christ into our lives, we were guilty of eternal death and total separation from God; but Jesus took the punishment for us.

Moreover, when we receive this redemptive grace, it *justifies* us before God, declaring us righteous through Jesus Christ if we receive Him into our hearts [Romans 5:1-2].

We believe and accept this blessing through faith in Jesus Christ [Romans 3:22-23].

Parallel to God's grace of unmerited favour, His redemptive grace, which brings salvation [Titus 2:11-14], is free to all who will accept it.

Redemptive grace releases us from the stronghold, and power of sin. It delivers us from eternal death, and frees us from the wrath of God.

We were dead in trespasses and sins [Ephesians 2:1-4]. Yet, God had mercy and compassion upon us because of His great love to everyone.

God's grace is limitless [II Corinthians 12:9], absolute, free, and there is no partiality.

He gives this grace to all who will accept His Son Jesus Christ.

God gave His Son freely, and whether we accept or reject Him, in order to receive redemptive grace, we must go through the path of faith.

Working our way to receive salvation through God's grace, or trying to purchase it will not do. We must receive this by faith [Romans 5:2].

Additionally, without the Holy Spirit bringing conviction to our hearts [John 8:9; Acts 2:37], we cannot experience redemptive grace.

To accept this grace we must also believe in the Virgin Birth of Jesus Christ [Luke 1:26-2].

This also includes Jesus' death, burial and resurrection [I Corinthians 15:1-5].

What is of significant importance is that we must believe that He is God's Son [Matthew 3:17] sent to reconcile fallen man back to Himself [II Corinthians 5:18].

Jesus became the mediator or intercessor [I John 2:1] between man and God.

Jesus was the One who went before God and negotiated our release from the bondage of sin.

He was willing to pay the ransom with His life so that we could be set free. This is God's expression of grace, unmerited favour towards mankind.

Redemptive grace, through Jesus Christ repaired the broken relationship between us and God.

Again, this grace can only be effective if we receive Jesus Christ into our hearts.

Since Jesus was able to appease [*pacify, relieve, and soften*] God, He opened the way for us.

Jesus' death was the only deed that could avert God's judgment from mankind.

Additionally, God will only accept the sinner, if that person believes in, and comes through the Blood of Jesus Christ.

The reason is that no one can enter the presence of God without first going through the blood of Jesus Christ.

His blood was shed to erase our sins because "...*without shedding of blood is no remission*" [Hebrews 9:22].

If the individual does not believe in the blood of Jesus, he or she cannot approach the Father.

Blood had to be shed to restore our relationship with God.

The only blood God would accept was that of His Son Jesus Christ.

Furthermore, Jesus' death justified us; thus excusing our inherited sins; again to escape God's wrath/judgment.

We accept God's redemptive grace by faith.

Chapter 5

A

Amazing Grace

Incredible, marvelous, remarkable, wonderful, miraculous…

God's grace is amazing because it took a special unusual kind of love and mercy that could save our sinful souls.

Think of the death of Jesus: cruel and shameful, even though He committed no sin [Isaiah 53:9; I Peter 2:22]. Yet, He was treated as a condemned man [Deuteronomy 25:3].

This is indeed amazing grace. It makes us *stop*, *step* back, and *think* about such great favour from Almighty God.

This is a marvelous, miraculous, and incredible gift from God through the obedience of Jesus Christ. He did not have to do it, but He did.

Yes, He sent His Son to this world to die out of love for us.

It may seem unbelievable that someone would even dare to offer a child to die for another. Yet God sent His Son to die to reconcile sinful man out of a life of depravity and from eternal death.

When we think of God's amazing grace, we should be willing and ready to forgive one another [Matthew 6:14, 15; 18:15-35].

God's love is really greater far than any author could pen; even if it took a million years.

The other feature of this amazing grace is that it will never diminish. In [II Corinthians 12:9 The Lord told Paul: *"My grace is sufficient for you"*].

God has a bountiful supply for all who will receive His grace.

God's grace is amazing because although we were His enemies because of Adam's sin; nevertheless

He reconciled us through the death of Jesus Christ [Romans 5:10a; 5:11].

This is wonderful and remarkable. *Amazing*!

In this world, we have to pay for our mistakes either in broken relationships or from the legal position.

Yet, while we were sinners Christ died for us [Romans 5:8]. It is truly unbelievable.

We can joy in the Lord Jesus because he atoned for our sins setting us free from the bondage of sin.

Jesus redeemed us from eternal death and made us sons and daughters in the kingdom of God with hope of eternal life.

Through Jesus, we are adopted in the Family of God [Romans 8:15-16].

Amazing grace re-establishes our relationship with God, and brings us into fellowship with Him and one another [I John 1:7].

This act of love was given all because of God's *unmerited favour*, the *redemptive grace* of giving His Son Jesus Christ through his death on Calvary for us, and His *amazing grace*.

It is God's amazing grace which gives us a new nature [II Peter 1:4] because we were by default, made the children of wrath as a result of sin (Ephesians 2:3).

However, upon acceptance of Jesus Christ into our hearts we became new creatures, and His divine nature is given to us with a new heart, and the right spirit.

This new nature frees us from condemnation after accepting salvation by faith (Romans 8:1).

God's amazing grace is truly wonderful, marvelous, incredible, and absolutely *amazing*.

Chapter 6

C

Christ-like Grace
A life of Self-discipline

*"For ye know the grace of our Lord Jesus Christ, that,
though he was rich, yet for sakes he became poor, that ye
through his poverty might be rich"*
(II Corinthians 8:9).

Christ-like grace speaks of love, care, humility,
meekness, selflessness, self-control, discipline,
forgiveness, and compassion [See Philippians 2:7-
8; Colossians 3:12-17].

When we receive God's Son through the gift of
salvation and begin to acknowledge His amazing
grace, we must express the change with Christ-like
attitudes [See Matthew 5], which will result in
Christian characteristics.

This motivates us to holy living and obedience to God's word to do His will.

The world cannot identify God's grace in us without our demonstration of love and humility.

The grace of the Lord Jesus Christ is expressed in humility because *"...though he was rich, yet for your sakes he became poor, that ye through his poverty might be rich."* [II Corinthians 8:9].

Additionally, He made Himself *"...of no reputation, and took upon Him the form of a servant, and was made in the likeness of men...He humbled Himself, and became obedient unto death, even the death of the cross"* (Philippians 2:7-8).

Jesus gave himself totally for the reconciliation of fallen man back to God.

He left his splendour in heaven to be born in a manger so that he could fulfill God's plan of redemption on Calvary's Cross.

Next, we look at Christ's disposition when he was under pressure, and His display of unconditional love.

While He awaited the Cross in the Garden of Gethsemane He prayed to the Father in earnest, *"...not my will, but thine be done."* [Luke 22:42].

When he was reviled by His accusers, He did not threaten, even after being severely beaten and shamed [I Peter 2:22-24].

Jesus took all the disparaging treatment with grace and humility.

This was indeed a true example of the fruit of the Spirit [Galatians 5:22-23].

Christ-like grace is the true expression of Christian dignity to endure persecution without issuing threats or seeking revenge.

Chapter 7

E

Enabling Grace
Sustaining Grace

*"And God is able to make all grace abound toward, you;
that ye, always having all sufficiency in all [things]. May
abound to every good work"*
(II Corinthians 9:8).

Enabling grace is administrative grace. It is working grace inspired through the anointing of the Holy Spirit. This makes it possible for us to do exploit for God even when under severe pressures.

By God's enabling grace, we will wait patiently upon Him for our appointed time during those experience of tests and trials [Job 14:14].

In the hour of temptation, it will be the enabling grace of God, which is sufficient [II Corinthians

12:9] that will keep us as the Holy Spirit empowers us with the anointing to under gird, and stabilize us so that we can be strong.

God's grace is made perfect in the hour of temptation and gives us strength as we have need.

It is when we are weak that we experience the creative and powerful grace of God.

Furthermore, during those times, God will make His grace compass us about *"as with a shield"* (Psalm 5:12).

Enabling grace is creative, because we do not always know what to do in trials; but God's grace will devise ways of overcoming those temptations.

God's enabling grace will give us strength in the hour of temptation and make us declare,

"How can I do this great wickedness, and sin against God" (Genesis 39:9b).

It is this kind of grace, which makes us say, *"If it be [so], our God whom we serve is able to deliver us from the burning fiery furnace, and he will deliver us out of thine hand, O king. But if not...we will not serve thy gods..."* [Daniel 3:17-18].

Enabling grace gives us supernatural strength to bear up under severe tests and trials.

This power comes through the use of the anointed and powerful armour of God [Ephesians 6:12-18].

It gives us courage to face giants, cross a Red Sea, go through a Jordan, and to overcome the fiery darts of the wicked one. Some troubles are similar to those situations.

Enabling grace is developed through constant communication with God, unceasing prayer [I Thessalonians 5:17], and listening to His voice [John 10:3-5] to obediently follow His commands.

Enabling grace makes us wait upon God even when He takes long to respond to our cry [Psalm 37:7, Luke 18:7].

Enabling grace will make us believe that God cares and delay to our prayers does not mean "no."

We need God's enabling grace to keep His commandments, to be obedient, and to do His will.

Moreover, God's enabling grace keeps us from falling into sin [Jude 24-25]. Nevertheless, we must rely upon God's wisdom and strength.

Still, even when we fall, we can trust His love, mercy, and faithfulness to forgive us from all our unrighteousness [I John 1:9-2:1].

It is only when by faith we give ourselves completely to God are we able to understand the efficacy of God's enabling grace.

God's grace of *unmerited favour*; His *redemptive grace*; His *amazing grace*; the *Christ-like grace*; and the *enabling grace* must all be received through faith in Jesus Christ.

God loves us with an everlasting love, and no one can separate us from this great love. *Amen.*

May the sweet and precious grace of Our Lord and Saviour Jesus Christ keep your hearts and minds in peace and joy.

Part II

Reflections on Grace

This section discusses the following themes:

1. The Truth about Jesus Christ

2. Expressive Grace

3. The Throne of Grace

4. The Spirit of Grace

5. Spiritual Development Grace

6. Super Abundant Grace

7. Special Needs Grace

8. The Gospel of Grace

Chapter 8

The Truth about Jesus Christ

Full of Grace and Truth

"And the Word was made flesh, and dwelt among us, (and we beheld his glory, the glory as of the only begotten of the Father,) full of grace and truth" John 1:14).

[Truth - Gk. Aletheia] means unveiled reality…the very essence of matter. It means reality, integrity, and accuracy.

What we see, read, and know about Jesus is all reality and truth and not mere appearance.

In I John 1:1-2, it says,

"That which was from the beginning, which we have heard, which we have seen with our eyes, which we have looked upon, and our hands have handled, of the Word of life.

For the life was manifested, [revealed] and we have seen it, and bear witness, and shew unto you that eternal life which was with the Father, and was manifested unto us..."

Jesus is real.

It is clear to see that Jesus is all truth without error, falsehood, or insincerity.

He is thoroughly full and complete with nothing lacking.

He is absolutely trustworthy and full of grace and uprightness.

The character of Jesus exposes sincerity, dependability, and faithfulness; thus displaying the very nature of grace.

Therefore, He is all integrity – full of truthfulness and the very essence of grace.

His character represents the expression of God's love and mercy towards mankind.

As we express the qualities and traits of Jesus Christ, our lives will be marked by truthfulness and faithfulness.

As Christians we must make every effort to apply the word of God in our witness to the world.

Therefore, our speech must always be "with grace" [Colossians 4:6].

When we allow the grace of Jesus Christ to manifest in our lives we will be free from offence.

Grace is a discipline to demonstrate every day as we live in this fallen world.

To be Christ-like is to endeavour to be like Him with the help of the Holy Spirit, as we dedicate our lives to Him.

Chapter 9

Expressive Grace

Jesus Revealed in the Flesh

"But when the fullness of the time was come, God sent forth his Son, made of a woman, made under the law,

To redeem them that were under the law, that we might receive the adoption of sons" (Galatians 4:4-5).

In this text we see that God revealed Himself as Jesus in the flesh. This was an expression of abounding grace in the demonstration of favour towards us. It was an expression of His great love towards mankind.

The expression of God's love is also very significant of His mercy even after man's disobedience.

We cannot be successful Christians without God's grace because we sin daily and come short of His glory.

Furthermore, when we willfully sin we separate ourselves from His presence. Yet, despite our failures, He is always ready to forgive.

According to [Psalm 86:5] *"For thou Lord, art good, and ready to forgive; and plenteous in mercy unto all them that call upon thee."*

Expressive grace displays kindness with dignified behaviour as we represent Jesus Christ in our lives.

With God's presence we can demonstrate these behaviours if we live in obedience to His word.

Moreover, when we are in His will, He gives us favour, which protects us and keeps us daily if we trust in Him.

According to Hebrews 4:16 *"Let us therefore come boldly unto the throne of grace, that we may obtain mercy, and find grace to help in time of need."*

God gives us abundant grace and expects us to display this virtue even in our speech. The word teaches,

"Let your speech be always with grace, seasoned with salt, that ye may know how ye ought to answer every man" [Colossians 4:6].

Obviously, a rich supply of grace will help us control our emotions so that we speak with humility and gentleness, rather than in arrogance or anger.

If our speech is graceful, we will respond through the Holy Spirit, instead of in our flesh.

Evidently, grace is expressed in our attitudes, behaviours, and the choice of words we use in our conversations (Proverbs 15:1).

The outcome is that we will be honest in our interactions with others, and in our business transactions.

There will be respect, integrity, purity, Christian conduct, and demeanour with no hidden agendas.

In order to maintain wholesome graceful speech especially in a disagreement, we must keep in mind Proverbs 15:1 *"A soft answer turns away wrath: but grievous words stir up anger."*

Grace can be effectively expressive when we acknowledge the favour of God in sending His Son to this earth to die for us [John 3:16].

The new believers in the early church did not simply accept God's bounty of grace.

Instead, they received it with gratitude and thanksgiving, in their acknowledgement of the absolute loving kindness and freeness of God.

Let us not take God's grace for granted. Even though it is free, we did not deserve it.

God's grace not only affects man's sinfulness through forgiveness, but it brings joy and thankfulness to him.

Now, this is why we should be eager to praise, worship, and testify of the love of God every opportunity we have when we think of God's redemptive grace.

Finally, we cannot express grace without the anointing of the Holy Spirit.

One of the ways in which we express grace is in our humility through the fruit of the Spirit [Galatians 5:22-23].

If we yield to God's will for our lives, He will bestow His grace to us.

According to Proverbs 3:34b *"He gives grace to the lowly."*

In James 4:6 we read, *"He gives more grace....God resists the proud, but gives grace unto humble"*

This is strength through enabling grace to *overcome temptation,* to *go through tests* and *fiery trials* without buckling or giving in to the flesh.

It would be impossible to overcome those experiences without a rich supply of God's grace.

[See II Corinthians 12:9 *"My grace is sufficient for you."*

Chapter 10

The Throne of Grace
Obtaining Help

*"Let is therefore come boldly unto the throne
of grace, that we may obtain mercy, and find
grace to help in time of need"*
[Hebrews 4:16].

Each time we approach God's presence, we are before His throne. When we do so, we must come in faith expecting to find mercy.

There should be no reservation in our hearts as to whether God will hear us, meet our needs, or accept us.

It takes grace through faith to approach a Holy God especially when we have sinned or strayed from Him.

Oh, the love and mercy of God toward us! Such love, that God should send His only Son, and still accept us when we sin against Him. This is incredible!

Let us draw near each time we go to Him with thankfulness, and adoration for such love.

At the throne of grace, we find *mercy, forgiveness, favour,* and *pardon,* and not judgment as we do in a court of law.

This is where we find our Mediator, Jesus Christ. Therefore, we need not be afraid when we enter His presence (Hebrews 12:24).

Such mercy and grace; completely different to *"the mount that might be touched, and that burned with fire...and the sound of trumpet, and the voice of words...and so terrible was the sight..."* (Hebrews 12:18-21).

As we approach His presence, let this be with praises, worship, and thanksgiving [Psalm 92:1, Philippians 4:6]. Instead of with doubts, fears and trembling.

If you truly love and trust God, you will not be afraid to approach Him at the *Throne of Grace* when you pray.

Jesus said, *"Men ought always to pray, and not to faint"* [Luke 18:1].

God expects us to go to Him, not only when we are in need, but as a daily discipline.

Chapter 11

The Spirit of Grace
The Holy Spirit

"Of how much sorer punishment, suppose ye, shall he be thought worthy, who hath trodden under foot the Son of God...and hath despite unto the Spirit of grace?" [Hebrews 10:29].

The Spirit of grace refers to the gift of the Holy Spirit, who indwells us.

Receiving Jesus Christ is accepting a combination of gifts of which grace is one of them [Ephesians 4:7].

These gifts are all from the Holy Spirit for *service* and *edification* for all believers [Ephesians 4].

The Holy Spirit in us makes us want to please God. He empowers us so that we want to express Christian qualities through the gift of grace.

Moreover, we will not be effective without the Holy Spirit being in control of our lives [Galatians 5:16].

When He is in control, our *character* will change, so that we can positively affect those around us. The hope is that our behaviour will influence them to accept Jesus Christ [Luke 1:17].

Through the Spirit of Grace, we develop *moral and spiritual qualities* to build Christian characters [Colossians 3:12-17; Galatians 5:22-26].

The Spirit of grace in us will enable us to flee corruptible behaviours if we daily submit to the Spirit and crucify the flesh.

However, if we neglect the gift of Salvation, we bring punishment unto ourselves because we show disdain to the Spirit of Grace [Hebrews 10:29].

Chapter 12

Spiritual Development
Nurturing Grace for Spiritual Growth

"But grow in grace, and [in] the knowledge of our Lord and Saviour Jesus Christ" [II Peter 3:18]

It is impossible for us to be successful in our Christian walk without the gift of grace.

We develop spiritual muscles through the grace of God.

Spiritual development of integrity, honesty, truthfulness, true commitment, and stability do not come from intellectualism or man's philosophy.

Assuredly, this knowledge does not come from cultural or personal ideologies. We can only obtain it through the grace of God.

Furthermore, growing in grace is a process, which leads into a deeper knowledge of God.

In any case, we must desire to know God to experience His grace.

Moreover, we receive grace as we have need. God does not give His grace in a casual fashion.

There must be a sincere desire for His grace.

As we have need for personal development and spiritual enrichment, we receive grace to develop into strong soldiers for the Lord.

Grace is not a license for sin [Romans 5:20].

Moreover, there will be consequences if we are indifferent to God's grace [Hebrews 10:29].

As we grow in the grace of Jesus Christ, we learn to live to please Him. It makes our lives blameless in the presence of those with whom we interact.

Chapter 13

Super Abundant Grace
Abounding Favour

And God [is] able to make all grace abound toward you; that ye, always having all sufficiency in all [things], may abound to every good work" [II Corinthians 9:8].

There are so many people today who are lacking the bare necessities of life.

They have need for clean water, safety, a roof over their heads, financial security and so many other things which those who have, and in some cases in excess take for granted.

Those persons who have plenty of the world's goods often seem reluctant to share.

For many, when they do, it is with exhibition for all to see, or grudgingly only because they want to write off their taxes.

Yet, God loves us so much that not only will He give us grace to save us, but abounding grace.

This grace far exceeds all our expectations and thoughts because of His great love toward us.

Super abundant grace is God's special generosity to those who will trust Him.

Nevertheless, there must be obedience, humility, submissiveness, and a willing heart to be committed to whatever He commands.

God does not give His grace capriciously on a whim. The individual must be totally surrendered to His will. There must be loyalty, confidence, reliability, and commitment.

The recipient must acknowledge through faith, that God will keep His word which is gone out of His mouth.

God's abounding grace will take us where nothing else could do.

Chapter 14
Special Needs Grace
Coping Grace

"And now for a little space grace hath been [shown] from the Lord our God, to leave us a remnant to escape, and to give us a nail in his holy place, that our God may lighten our eyes, and give us a little reviving in our bondage"
[Ezra 9:8].

"Let us therefore come boldly unto the throne of grace, that we may obtain mercy, and find grace to help in the time of need"
[Hebrews 4:16].

Everyone at some time or another will face painful situations when the need for special grace is required.

These are times of severe trials, and temptations from various sources.

During those instances it seems as if there is no end to trials and troubles.

Nevertheless, we need not fear because God will give us grace to help us so that we do not go under and succumb to those situations.

"But he gives more grace. Wherefore he saith, ['God resists the proud, but gives grace unto the humble']" James 4:6.

Have you ever said to yourself *"Lord, give me grace"* in a moment of stress?

It is at such times when God's coping grace takes on its role as comforter, strength, and support.

You may wonder at times "How did I ever make it through those hard times."

"I thought I would have never made it through."

It was on those occasions of needed grace when God extends His special favour so that we can cope with the trying circumstances of life.

Another point is when we are going through the desert experience.

There is the tendency to think that God has forsaken us [Psalm 42, 43], or that He has turned His back upon us.

This will not happen because it is during those situations that we excel if we trust His grace to take us through.

Special needs grace is coping grace which will support the leader who discovers wantonness, and willfulness of sin in the church.

That person will go before God for the people as Ezra did [Ezra 9:5-9]. God will hear and He will forgive. As leaders we cannot ignore sin in the camp.

God is faithful, but we must draw from His faithfulness and trust Him to deliver and forgive our sins.

We can make it through temptations and trials if we depend and rely upon God's grace during our times of need.

Grace will help us to cope with self-control and discipline, in order to overcome the power of sin and escape its consequences.

Chapter 15
The Gospel of Grace
Salvation to all Mankind

"For by grace are ye saved through faith;
and that not of yourselves: it is the gift of
God: Not of works, lest any man should
boast" [Ephesians 2:8-9]

The gospel of grace is the only doctrinal teachings that can save and bring us into relationship with God. This was divinely inspired [II Timothy 3:16; II Peter 1:20-21] with all the attributes necessary for spiritual and natural growth and development.

The reason is that when an individual receives this grace, it changes the entire life for the glory of God.

Furthermore, the gospel of grace refers to the free salvation God gives to whosoever will accept it through His Son Jesus Christ.

According to Paul

"For the grace of God that brings salvation hath appeared to all men, Teaching us that, denying ungodliness and worldly lusts, we should live soberly, righteously, and godly, in this present world" [Titus 2:11-12].

The gospel of grace is the message of salvation offered to the sinner as the Holy Spirit convicts him of sins.

When the individual acknowledges sin, confession will be made from the heart in readiness to accept Jesus Christ (Romans 10:9-10).

However, this work is not complete because there must be a sincere desire to live holy and righteously for the Lord. It is a continuous work of sanctification in the life of the believer.

Besides, Paul shows us that we can live holy lives if we walk in the Spirit [Galatians 5:16].

The gospel of grace, when received will bring about repentance and a change from dead works to live righteously for the Lord.

Other Publications

Dr Stuart is an avid writer and has published the following books:

Betrayal of Sacred Trust

Available at iUniverse, Barnes & Noble and Amazon.com

This book relates to those who have experienced adultery in their marriages.

It is the product of a doctoral research on women who are living or have lived with husbands who have committed adultery during their marital relationship.

There are excerpts to the response/reaction of the women on the discovery of adultery.

Do not miss purchasing your copy.

What others are saying about
Betrayal of Sacred Trust

When I read the book I saw myself and wished I had this information before I went forward to divorce to my husband...

I use this book in my counseling sessions both pre-marital and marriage...

This book brings awareness to the consequences of adultery and how it tears a family apart and hurt the deceived spouse...

I would encourage everyone to read this book for enlightenment and understanding concerning the consequences of adultery...

The writer took time to explore the emotional and spiritual consequences of adultery and how it affects the entire family...

This is a must read...

TEN Questions to Ask Myself before I say I DO
Available at Amazon.com and Createspace.com

TEN Qs is a manual for the preparation of marriage.

TEN Qs is a book for those who accept the sacredness of holy matrimony the way God intended.

This book is required reading for the counselor, youth leader, pastor, singles, mother and daughter, group and retreat study, and Sunday School discussion.

What others are saying about TEN Qs

You have mentioned situations I am sure a lot of us have not even thought of before taking this sacred step in life...

I suggest this book be read by each person who is in a relationship and plans to marry...

The book clearly explains some interesting scenes you will encounter while you are dating and also after marriage...

I enjoyed reading the following topics: "Who am I"; "Requirements for Marriage;" "Getting to know him/her;" "What am I looking for;" and "Compatibility"...

Books Available at

www.themarriagecorner.web.officelive.com

And Amazon.com

The Power of Prayer

Principles of Spiritual Leadership

Managing difficult People

Fruit of the Spirit

Workplace Abuse

What is Love

Spiritual Warfare

Made in the USA
Charleston, SC
17 May 2010